CW00855198

INNOVATORS ADVANCING MEDICINE

Robyn Hardyman

LUCENT
PRESS

Published in 2020 by
Lucent Press, an Imprint of Greenhaven Publishing, LLC
353 3rd Avenue
Suite 255
New York, NY 10010

Produced for Lucent by Calcium
Designers: Paul Myerscough and Simon Borrough
Picture researcher: Rachel Blount
Editors: Sarah Eason and Jennifer Sanderson

Picture credits: Shutterstock: Levent Konuk; Inside: Carnegie Mellon University: p. 41; Harvard Biodesign Lab: Rolex Awards/Fred Merz: pp. 1cl, 42, 43; Himore Medical Equipments: p. 27bl; Medrobotics: p. 5; Medtronic, Inc.: Reproduced with permission of Medtronic, Inc.: p. 25cr; MinXray, Inc.: p. 6; Peek Vision: (c) Rolex / Joan Bardeletti: p. 13; Jacob Arthur Pritchard/The Rockefeller University: p. 36; Seismic: p. 38; Sensible Medical: p. 29; Shutterstock: Andrey_Popov: p. 3, 14; Anton_Ivanov: p. 10; Ase: p. 24; BlueRingMedia: p. 22; ChameleonsEye: p. 7; Ivan Chudakov: p. 37; Design_Cells: p. 35; Digital Images Studio: p. 19; Elnur: pp. 1r, 21, 39; Fotocrisis: p. 45; Illustration Forest: p. 20; Jasni: p. 27br; Puwadol Jaturawutthichai: p. 17; Kateryna Kon: p. 30; Lightspring: p. 25b; MAD.vertise: p. 26; Microgen: p. 31; Minerva Studio: pp. 1cr, 15; Monkey Business Images: pp. 1l, 28, 34; Nokwalai: p. 32; Petarg: p. 33; Photo Oz: p. 40; Robert Przybysz: p. 23; Joseph Sohm: p. 12; Travel Stock: p. 4; Suzanne Tucker: p. 16; Tukaram.Karve: p. 11; Vitstudio: p. 44; Sherry Yates Young: p. 18; Vaxxas: pp. 9t, 9b; Wikimedia Commons: Hdptcar: p. 8.

Cataloging-in-Publication Data

Names: Hardyman, Robyn.
Title: Innovators advancing medicine / Robyn Hardyman.
Description: New York : Lucent Press, 2020. | Series: Earth's innovators | Includes glossary and index.
Identifiers: ISBN 9781534565425 (pbk.) | ISBN 9781534565432 (library bound) | ISBN 9781534565449 (ebook)
Subjects: LCSH: Medical technology--Juvenile literature. | Medical innovations--Juvenile literature.
Classification: LCC R855.4 H37 2020 | DDC 610.28--dc23

Printed in the United States of America

CPSIA compliance information: Batch #BS19KL:
For further information, contact Greenhaven Publishing, LLC, New York, New York, at 1-844-317-7404.

Please visit our website, www.greenhavenpublishing.com.
For a free color catalog of all our high-quality books, call toll free 1-844-317-7404 or fax 1-844-317-7405.

Contents

CHAPTER 1

DELIVERING GLOBAL HEALTH CARE

Over the past 100 years, we have made many amazing advances in our understanding of diseases and our ability to treat them. This has made it possible for people to live longer than ever before. We have made great strides in technology, too. We have combined all these innovations to help improve the health care we can deliver.

We still face a big challenge, however, to provide adequate health care for everybody. The world's population is growing and, as people live longer, their medical needs become more complex. In many of the poorer areas of the world, people do not have access to even the most basic levels of care. They live too far away from any health care provider, and they cannot afford to pay for what is available. All this needs to change. Innovators are working on every aspect of this challenge.

People living in remote areas of poorer countries may not have access to health care. These women are attending a clinic in India.

They are striving to develop the technology to improve health care for both the wealthier and the poorer countries of the world.

Robot Physician

One of the most cutting-edge areas of innovation in health care is robotics. A robot is a machine that can be programmed, or instructed, to do a job. Some, such as robots on an automobile assembly line, work entirely without human control. In medicine, robots like these are now being used to dispense medication in hospital pharmacies, for example, and to handle samples in research laboratories.

Throat Surgery

Recent technology has developed robots that can work in an operating room. The robots, which perform some functions independently and some when directed by a surgeon, can be used to reach inaccessible parts of the body. Flex is the name of a robot that operates on the throat. Its flexible tube is inserted down the patient's throat and guided by a surgeon, using a joystick. A camera on the end shows what is inside. Once Flex reaches the site to be operated on, it stiffens to create a stable platform for its kit of surgical instruments. Controlling Flex with the help of its camera, the surgeon can cut out a lump or stitch an internal wound. Without Flex, surgeons would have to break the patient's jaw or cut open their neck to access these areas.

Robotic systems like Flex are making it possible for surgeons to develop new techniques in surgery.

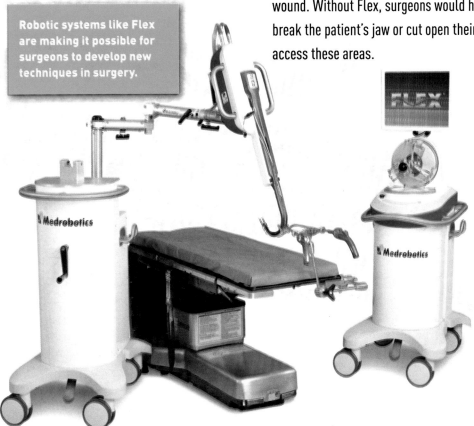

Medical Advances for Developing Countries

In remote areas of developing countries, people often cannot access health care. Clinics and hospitals may be located hours away from where people live and they many have no transportation. Clinics may also have limited supplies of medication, equipment, and power. These problems have influenced many recent innovations in medicine, such as making portable medical equipment that is lightweight yet strong, and that can be used in areas where there is no electricity.

Diagnosis

The first stage in delivering successful medicine is correctly diagnosing the patient's problem. One way of doing this is using X-rays. X-ray machines are usually expensive, large, and heavy, but one innovative company, MinXray, has developed the CMDR-25, a portable X-ray device. It is built onto a two-wheel cart, and can fit in the back of a regular car.

The CMDR-25 is easily portable, so it can easily be transported to clinics in developing countries, wherever it is needed.

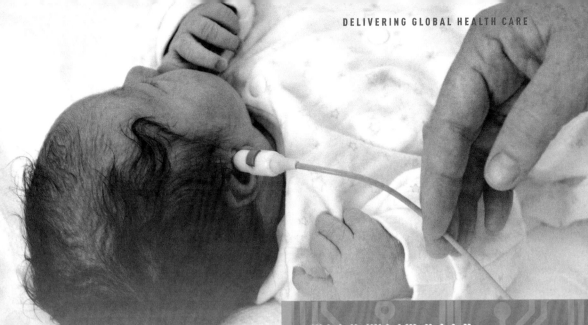

This newborn baby is being screened for any hearing problems.

Screening

Every year, about 500,000 babies are born around the world with impaired hearing. This problem is worse in the developing world. For example, in India, each year, about 100,000 babies are born with impaired hearing. In the developed world, babies' hearing is routinely tested and any problems are picked up. In about 40 low-income and 53 low- to middle-income countries, routine testing has been too expensive and difficult. Nitin Sisodia is an Indian electrical engineer who has devised a cheaper way of screening babies' hearing in developing countries. With his Sohum hearing device, any problems can be detected early, and treatment can be given to babies before they become worse.

INGENIOUS INNOVATIONS

Transporting and storing medications in low-income countries and hot climates is another problem innovators are solving. Many medications need to be kept cool to be effective. This is especially true of vaccines, which are given to people to protect them from diseases. One German innovator, Julia Römer, has developed Coolar. Coolar is a refrigerator for vaccines and other medications that does not need electricity to work. It is powered by hot water, which is heated by the sun. Coolar can last a long time because it has no moving parts, and is kind to the environment because it contains no hazardous cooling fluids. This innovation will enable health professionals to preserve lifesaving medicines and vaccines in a reliable and eco-friendly way. Coolar has been recognized for its excellence, winning a 2018 award from Startup Energy Transition, the leading international platform supporting innovation in energy.

7

Nanopatch

Vaccinating children against common but serious infectious diseases has saved millions of lives. Vaccination programs have also made a massive contribution to the overall improvement in people's health around the world. In poorer countries, however, it can be difficult to reach enough of the population with vaccinations in order to protect them. Vaccination programs are expensive, and it can be hard for doctors and nurses to get to people in remote areas.

Challenging Technology

Not only are vaccines expensive to produce and to transport to where they are needed, but they also need to be kept cool throughout their journey. This can be very difficult in countries where access to refrigeration is poor. If they become warm, the vaccines spoil and no longer work. Also, the vaccines are injected into a person's muscle using a needle and syringe, and keeping a supply of clean needles is expensive. One innovator was determined to overcome the problems with conventional vaccines. He is Professor Mark Kendall, an Australian biomedical engineer. Professor Kendall developed the Nanopatch, which is a revolutionary new method for delivering a vaccine.

In developing countries, vaccine programs are often limited by poor roads, climate, and lack of money.

Skin Deep

The Nanopatch is a tiny patch that is stuck onto the person's skin and left in place for just a few seconds. Thousands of tiny spikes on the surface of the patch are coated in a dose of the vaccine, and they deliver it to just under the person's skin. That is enough to protect them from the disease.

There are many advantages to the Nanopatch. The vaccination process is almost completely painless, and because the skin is not deeply pierced by a needle, there is lower risk of any infection. The patches use much less vaccine than the conventional method—as little as 1 percent of the amount—which means that many more people can be vaccinated at a lower overall cost. The patches are also very cheap to make, at less than $1 each. Very importantly, the vaccine is in the form of a dry coating on the patch, instead of a liquid, so it does not have to be kept cool. It works even in hot climates, so there is no need for expensive refrigeration in its transportation and storage.

World Class

When the first trials of the Nanopatch had spectacular success, Professor Kendall founded a company called Vaxxas to develop his product. Vaxxas has attracted the attention of the Centers for Disease Control and Prevention (CDC) and World Health Organization (WHO), among many other health bodies, and the company is currently doing human clinical trials, or tests on people, so that this groundbreaking innovation can start saving more lives.

CHAPTER 2

TELEMEDICINE

In the last decade, one development in technology has made a big difference to people's ability to access health care. Around the world, and even in the poorest countries, most people now carry a cell phone. This device has made it possible for billions more people to be connected to the Internet and to each other, and now, innovators are using this technology to deliver medical services to even the most remote regions.

Mothers and Babies

Herve Dongmo is an engineer and innovator at GiftedMom, an award-winning enterprise that develops low-cost technologies to improve the health of mothers and their young children in Cameroon, Africa. During their pregnancy, women receive text and voice messages on their cell phones to remind them when they need to attend a care appointment. After they have given birth, the mothers continue to receive these messages so they know when their baby needs a vaccination or a health check. The messages also teach them healthy habits to look after themselves and their babies.

It is important for women to have access to good health care throughout pregnancy and after the birth of their baby.

Another award-winning innovation for babies is Khushi Baby. Ruchit Nagar, an Indian innovator, started Khushi Baby as a class project while studying at the Yale School of Public Health in Connecticut. Khushi Baby is a digital necklace, which babies wear to manage their health. An app on the mother's phone runs Khushi Baby. A health-care worker simply scans the necklace with their phone to access the baby's health records, and can input information such as dates for vaccination and the state of the baby's health. Physicians and other health care workers can access this information, too. The system also automatically calls mothers in their local language to remind them when vaccinations are due. Khushi Baby has been trialed in hundreds of villages in India, and is now set for expansion.

Doctor on Demand

In Côte d'Ivoire, West Africa, Serge Koffi is also using telemedicine for local people's health. He is the cofounder of MedecinDirect, a medical helpline that is accessed by phone from anywhere in the region. It enables people to consult a physician on any issue related to their health or that of their family. Serge Koffi is one of the 40 best young African innovators recognized by Africa4Tech, an international organization working to provide innovative solutions to problems in Africa.

> **Digital technology has made it possible to reach far more people with health care, and to monitor their health needs at all stages of their lives.**

Sharing Expert Knowledge

Phone technology is being used to connect people in remote areas with the physicians and nurses who can deliver medical services to them. It is also being used to train those medical professionals. The WHO estimates the world will need about 12.9 million more health professionals by 2035. The expert knowledge of experienced physicians and nurses can now be handed down to new generations who are in training, even in the most remote areas.

Training Local Workers

One project, led by researchers at the Oxford University in the United Kingdom (U.K.) has developed cell phone technology to support and improve the work of local health workers in Kenya, East Africa. These health workers are volunteers, so they need training. They also need the tools to decide on the health care needs of local children under the age of five. The team has developed a package to support them. This includes facts that they need to know and a way to record the health data that they collect in the community. This data is automatically sent to their supervisors. This technology helps the local health workers decide which children need to see a doctor or nurse, so they can get the care they need.

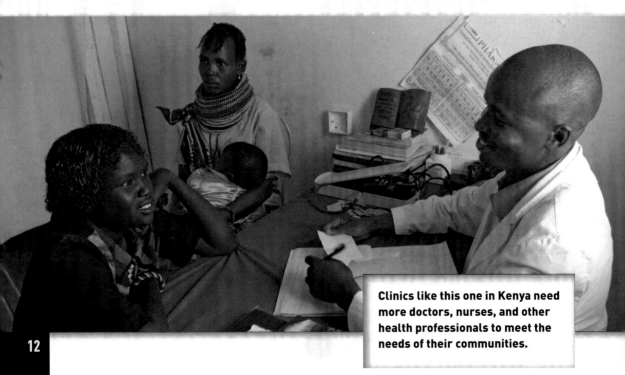

Clinics like this one in Kenya need more doctors, nurses, and other health professionals to meet the needs of their communities.

Finding Hidden Problems

An unexpected result of the project has been that it has identified many children with disabilities. It is thought that their mothers had been afraid to ask for help because of some local people's hostile attitudes toward disability. The result was that their children's needs were not being met. Now a new project called Hidden Children is supporting those children and their mothers, and raising awareness of the issue in Kenya.

INGENIOUS INNOVATIONS

Poor eyesight affects millions of people in developing countries. It can keep them from studying, working, and raising their living standards. Too often, no treatment is available. One British eye surgeon, Andrew Bastawrous, has pioneered a solution: a portable eye test kit that operates by cell phone. It is called Peek the Portable Eye Examination Kit and it can be used by ordinary people to scan eyes for the most common eye diseases. The results of the scans are sent to trained eye doctors in distant hospitals, who decide on the best treatment. Peek is now used in Kenya, Botswana, Tanzania, Ethiopia, and India, and there are plans for further expansion.

These trained volunteers are using Peek in Nakuru, Kenya, to test the vision and eye health of local children.

ClickMedix

As a graduate student at Massachusetts Institute of Technology (MIT), Ting Shih was set the challenge of creating a business that would impact more than 1 billion people. She knew she wanted it to be in health care. It seemed to her that more people in developing countries had access to a cell phone than to electricity, so she decided to use phones as the means to reach them. The result was ClickMedix.

Connecting Doctors and Patients

ClickMedix is a software program that helps health professionals serve more patients while lowering their costs. Health care workers use it to get expert advice from remote specialists. Even family members with no training can use the program on their phone to send health information and photos to a doctor.

Patients and health care workers can access the expert knowledge of a doctor from their phone.

14

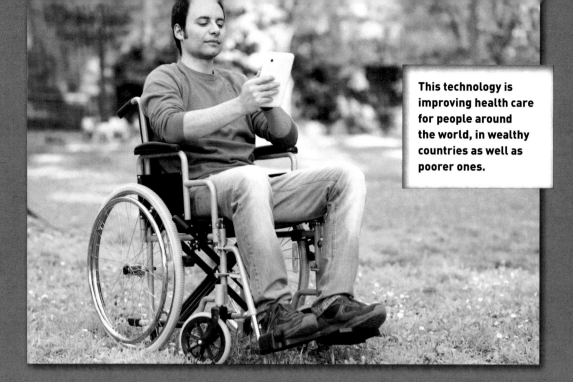

Ting and her team spent three years developing and trialing ClickMedix. They started in some of the poorest countries, as the hardest test. In Egypt, Uganda, Ghana, and Guatemala, for example, it was used to diagnose skin problems and diseases. In Peru, the Philippines, and China, it was used for monitoring the health of pregnant women, new mothers, and their babies. In China and the Philippines it was also used for the health care needs of the elderly.

In the United States

The results of ClickMedix's first projects were very encouraging. When people in the United States heard of its success, they wanted to see it in use there, too. There is always a drive to reach more people with health care, in the most effective way, while keeping costs down. ClickMedix is now partnering with several health care providers to deliver health care services for skin problems and other issues in clinics across the country, from California to Illinois to Virginia.

Around the World

This innovative project has been used worldwide to reduce the wait time for patients to see a physician from months to fewer than 72 hours. The system allows physicians to serve up to 15 times more patients, and has improved the lives of more than 350,000 people. It also trains the people who use it, which is more than 2,000 health professionals. This creates a more skilled workforce and new jobs for the community. A third benefit is that ClickMedix has saved health care providers millions of dollars, money that can be spent on providing health care to even more people.

CHAPTER 3

GLOBAL DISEASES

About 60 million people die each year around the world. It is a fact of life that we will all die one day, though we hope for a long and healthy life. The causes of those deaths vary between the wealthiest and the poorest countries. This is because people's lifestyles and their access to health care vary so much. There are some diseases, however, that we know are the biggest killers right across the globe. The fight is on to combat these and to reduce their impact on our lives.

Lifestyle Diseases

Some of the biggest killers around the world are not infectious diseases. Rather, they are the result of our lifestyles. This means factors such as what we eat and drink, and how much we exercise. Lifestyle diseases and conditions include heart disease, stroke, lung disease, and some types of diabetes and cancer. Lack of exercise and poor diet can lead to heart disease and stroke. A stroke is when a blood vessel leaks in the brain. It is often caused by having

Being obese, or being very overweight, increases a person's chances of developing a whole range of serious diseases.

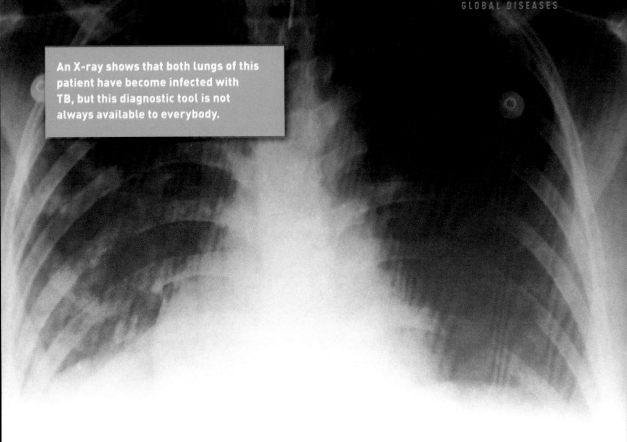

An X-ray shows that both lungs of this patient have become infected with TB, but this diagnostic tool is not always available to everybody.

high blood pressure. Lung disease is usually caused by smoking. A diet high in sugary foods can lead to diabetes. So the first innovation here needs to come from us. We must make healthy choices for ourselves, to keep us well. For the millions of people who suffer from these diseases, however, innovators are working on solutions to improve their treatment.

Tuberculosis

Tuberculosis (TB) is an infectious disease that can be caught from infected people via droplets in the air when they cough. It produces swellings in the lungs. Around the world, TB causes about 1.5 million deaths each year. With the right medication, however, TB is very treatable. Between 2000 and 2016, an estimated 53 million lives were saved through quick TB diagnosis and treatment. However, TB can be hard to diagnose. For many years, a skin test has been the standard method of diagnosis, but this cannot tell the difference between someone with the disease and someone who has been vaccinated against it. A team at Oxford University has come up with a new test. The team's T-Spot test is quicker, as well as being more sensitive and accurate. It is becoming widely used in the fight against TB.

The Big Ones

Today, the war that modern science and medicine are fighting against disease is highly sophisticated. Researchers and physicians are using the very latest cutting-edge technologies to find ways to combat the diseases that cause the most suffering and death around the world.

Influenza

Most people catch influenza (flu) at some time in their lives. If we are generally healthy, it takes a week or two to get over the fever and the aches, then we return to normal. For millions of people around the world, however, flu is a killer. If you are very young or very old, or your health is already not great, it can kill you by causing an infection in your lungs called pneumonia. Flu also spreads quickly, infecting millions of people at once. Innovators are working hard to find ways to combat this hidden killer.

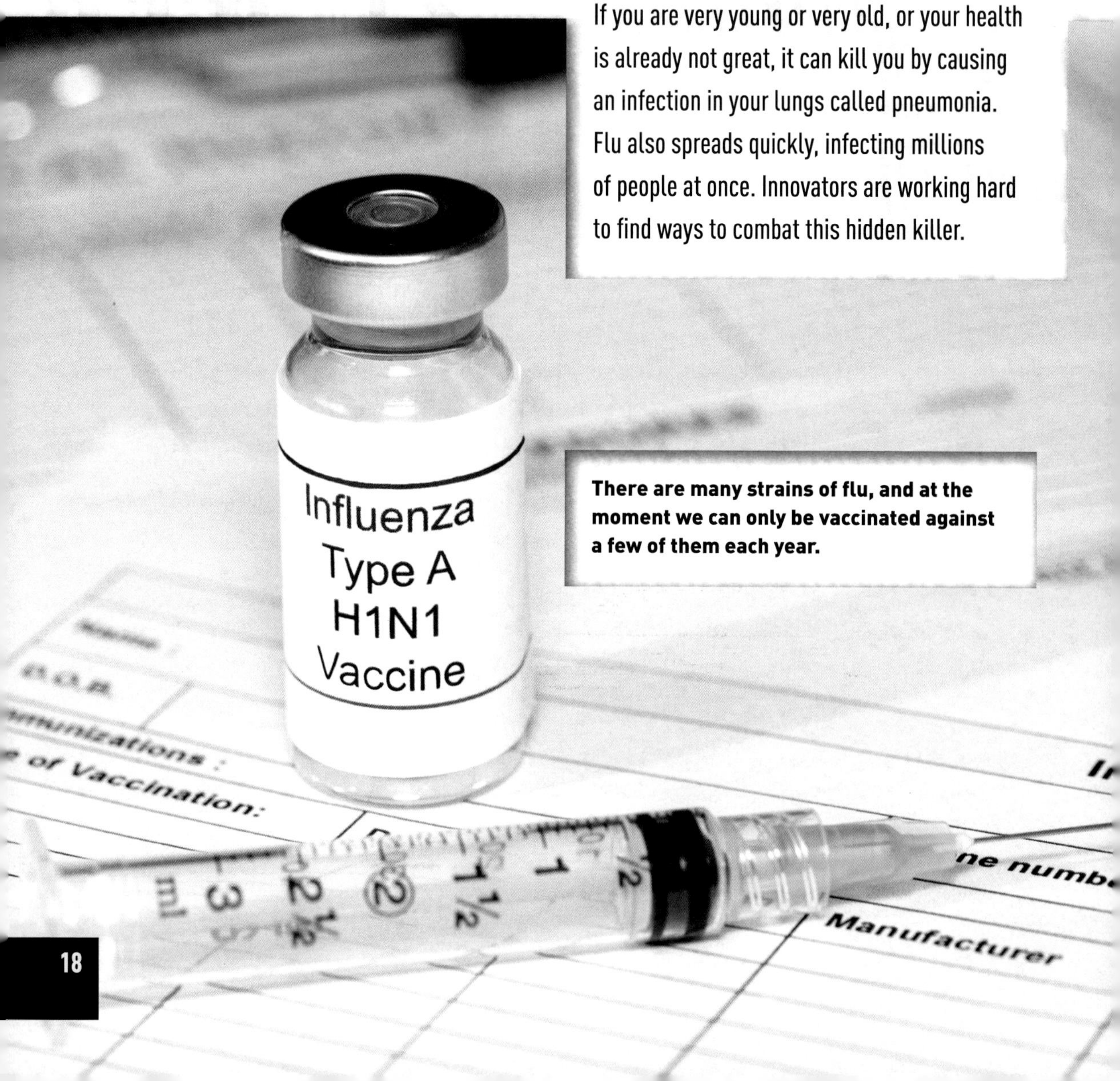

There are many strains of flu, and at the moment we can only be vaccinated against a few of them each year.

Influenza
Type A
H1N1
Vaccine

We can be vaccinated against the flu, but only against the strains, or types, of it that we know of. Each year, new strains emerge around the world. The search is on for a universal flu vaccine, meaning one that could protect us against all flu types, forever.

Peter Palese and his team at the Icahn School of Medicine in New York City have at last produced the first ever universal vaccine, which is currently being tested in clinics. If successful, this could save many millions of lives worldwide.

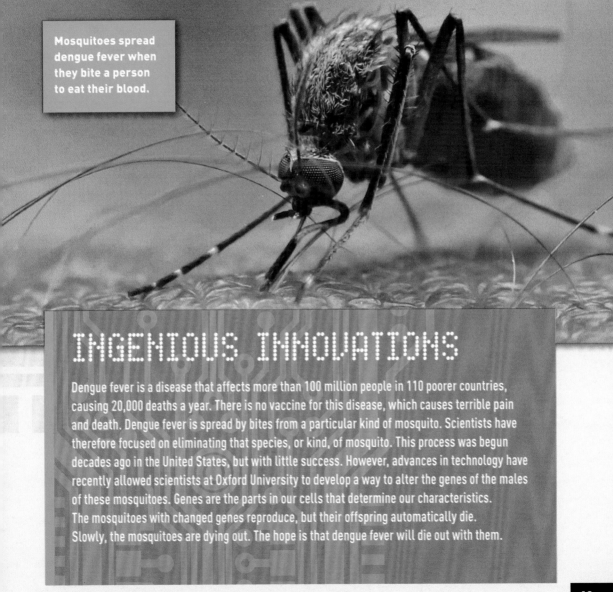

Mosquitoes spread dengue fever when they bite a person to eat their blood.

INGENIOUS INNOVATIONS

Dengue fever is a disease that affects more than 100 million people in 110 poorer countries, causing 20,000 deaths a year. There is no vaccine for this disease, which causes terrible pain and death. Dengue fever is spread by bites from a particular kind of mosquito. Scientists have therefore focused on eliminating that species, or kind, of mosquito. This process was begun decades ago in the United States, but with little success. However, advances in technology have recently allowed scientists at Oxford University to develop a way to alter the genes of the males of these mosquitoes. Genes are the parts in our cells that determine our characteristics. The mosquitoes with changed genes reproduce, but their offspring automatically die. Slowly, the mosquitoes are dying out. The hope is that dengue fever will die out with them.

Cancer

Cancer is the second biggest cause of death in the world, after heart disease and stroke. This disease causes cells in the body to grow rapidly in an uncontrolled way to form lumps called tumors. These tumors then interfere with the healthy workings of the body. If they are not treated, the patient dies. Sometimes, even the treatments we do have are not enough to defeat the disease.

A Many-Headed Monster

Cancer is not really one disease, it is hundreds of different versions of the same problem of abnormal cell growth. Our lifestyle causes some types. Most cases of lung cancer, for example, are caused by smoking. Being overweight can also make some cancers more likely to develop. But often cancer happens for reasons we cannot identify. Recent innovations in cancer diagnosis and treatment are focused on understanding the differences between the cancer types, and targeting them specifically.

Normally when we become sick, our immune system fights the infection. Cancer, however, can produce signals that switch off our immune system. Innovators are working on ways to switch the immune system back on, so our natural defenses can go on the attack. The two main ways to do this are with a vaccine and drugs.

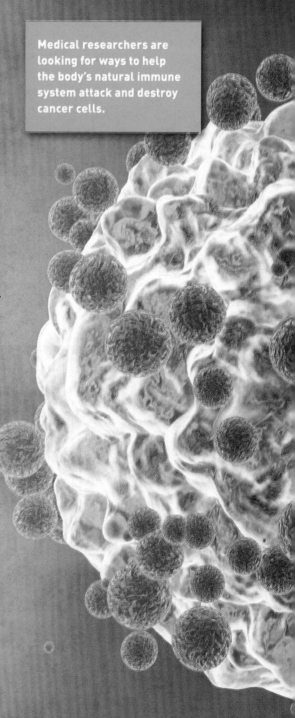

Medical researchers are looking for ways to help the body's natural immune system attack and destroy cancer cells.

20

Advances are being made to help us find ways to allow more and more people to recover from cancer.

Searching for Vaccines

Vaccines that attack cancer are different from the normal injections we get. They are not given to well people to protect them from the disease. Instead, they are given to people with cancer, to kick-start their immune systems. Researchers at Stanford University have made a vaccine that worked well on destroying the cancers in mice in laboratories. It is now being tested on people. Catherine Wu, a researcher at Harvard Medical School in Massachusetts, also led a team that produced an effective vaccine for a small group of six patients with skin cancer. These vaccines are very specific to the type of tumor they are treating.

Finding Cancer

Diagnosing cancer in its early stages is one of the most important factors in being able to cure it. With more than 200 different types of cancer, it is hard for doctors to spot all the possible signs of cancer in a 10-minute appointment. One new piece of technology created by two doctors in London, U.K., is designed to help. Called C the Signs, it is available as an app or online. It allows the doctor to enter patients' symptoms and, in fewer than 30 seconds, see what tests or urgent appointments with specialist doctors they may need. This simple tool could get many people into lifesaving treatment faster.

iLet

Diabetes is a disease that is causing big problems in the United States and other wealthy countries. More than 30 million Americans suffer from it, or about 9 percent of the population. Diabetics are more likely to develop heart disease and have strokes.

Types of Diabetes

Most people develop diabetes as adults, as a result of eating an unhealthy diet and becoming very overweight, or obese. This is Type 2 diabetes. However, there is a second type of diabetes that is not related to lifestyle, which develops in childhood. This is Type 1 diabetes.

Controlling Blood Sugar

People with diabetes have too much sugar in their blood. The system in the body that normally controls blood sugar fails. In a healthy person, an organ of the body called the pancreas produces insulin, a substance that removes the sugar from blood. Type 1 diabetics cannot produce any insulin, so they must inject themselves with it. They need to keep a careful watch on their blood sugar levels, so they know when they need an injection. This challenge has attracted the attention of one remarkable innovator, Edward Damiano, a professor of biomedical engineering at Boston University. Professor Damiano and his team at Boston have a developed the iLet.

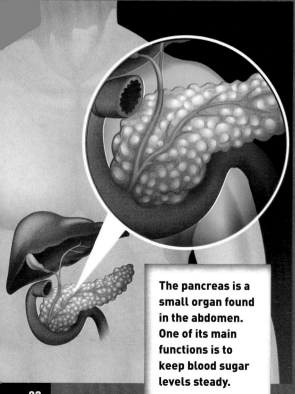

The pancreas is a small organ found in the abdomen. One of its main functions is to keep blood sugar levels steady.

It's Personal

The iLet is a pocket-sized device for diabetics to wear. It measures the sugar levels in the wearer's blood, and automatically delivers insulin to the body when it is needed, 24 hours a day. Users input information such as when they have had a meal, and if it was large or small.

Professor Damiano had a very personal reason to search for a way to help Type 1 diabetics regulate their blood sugar. His son developed Type 1 diabetes as an infant and, as his son grew, Professor Damiano saw how the management of his condition was difficult, complex, and tiring not just for his son, but for the whole family. He therefore aimed to invent a device that could manage blood sugar automatically by the time his son was old enough to go to college. And that is exactly what he did.

Trials and Tests

The iLet is currently undergoing clinical trials. These trials are showing remarkable results, with dramatic improvements in the blood sugar levels of people with Type 1 diabetes. The producers of iLet are seeking official approval, and Professor Damiano hopes that this innovative device will be in use by 2020.

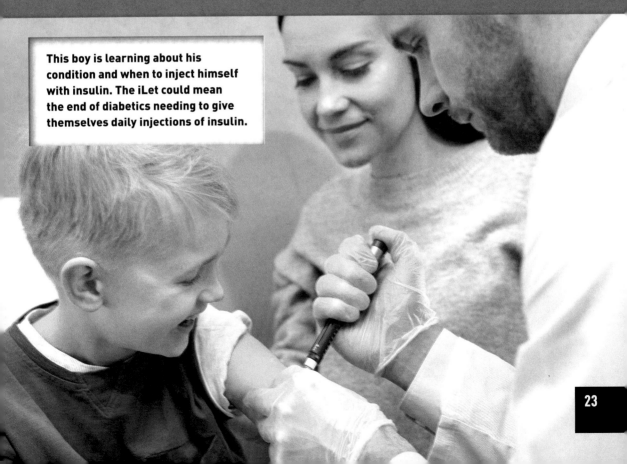

This boy is learning about his condition and when to inject himself with insulin. The iLet could mean the end of diabetics needing to give themselves daily injections of insulin.

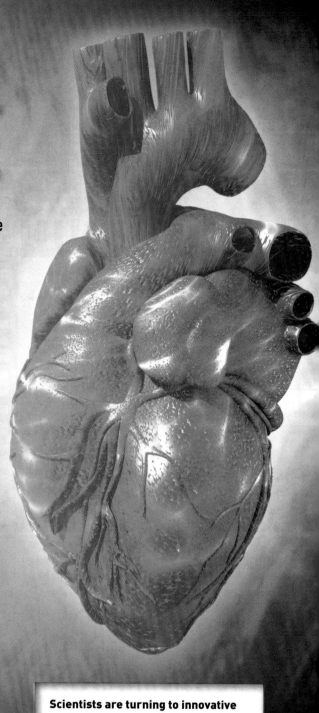

CHAPTER 4

HEART DISEASE

Heart disease is the leading cause of death in the United States. It is responsible for one in four deaths every year. Almost 6 million Americans currently have heart failure, which means their heart cannot pump blood around the body properly. Across the developed world, the problem is the same, so the need for innovation in this area is urgent. Fortunately, technology is bringing exciting advances all the time.

New Drugs

Researchers in the pharmaceutical industry, which develops new medicines, are working hard to find new ways to treat patients with heart problems. About 200 new medicines are in development in the United States alone. Another innovation is being used to test these and other medicines. Many new drugs are never made because tests show they have a harmful effect on the heart, making it beat in an irregular pattern. Scientists at Oxford University have developed a computer model of the heart, which can show the effect of

Scientists are turning to innovative medical devices to lengthen the life of patients with heart failure.

the drugs while they are still in an early stage of development. They are working with the big pharmaceutical companies to save them precious time and money.

A Regular Beat

Pacemakers have been used for patients with an irregular heartbeat for decades. A pacemaker is a small device inserted under the skin, with electrical wires running to the heart. It sends a weak electric current along the wires to the heart to control its beating, making it regular. The pacemaker's wires can stop working or cause infection in the body, so health care firm Medtronic has come up with a pacemaker that has no wires.

The wireless pacemaker is tiny, hardly bigger than a dime. It is inserted into a blood vessel in the patient's leg. From there, it is guided up through the body in the large blood vessels, until it reaches the heart. There, it is inserted directly into the heart, where it gives out an electric signal that controls the heart's beating. There is no need for the patient's chest to be cut open. This is really important, as large wounds like that take a long time to heal and can become infected.

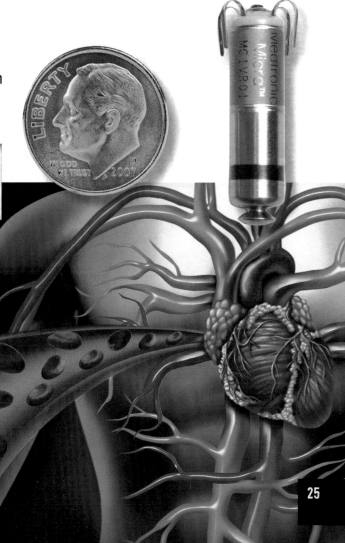

The wireless pacemaker is not much bigger than a dime, and no major surgery is needed to insert it.

Heart Health

Innovators in both wealthy and poorer nations are addressing the challenges of heart disease in their countries.

Blood Vessels

Sometimes there is no alternative to surgery on the heart. For example, children who have certain heart defects may need surgery to replace the blood vessels connecting the heart to the lungs. The artificial blood vessels that are currently used in these surgeries are made of a material that cannot grow as the child grows. This means they have to have repeated surgery every few years. Now, however, Robert Tranquillo, a professor of biomedical engineering at the University of Minnesota, and his team have invented artificial blood vessels that can grow inside the body. It is still the early days for this innovative technology, but it looks exciting.

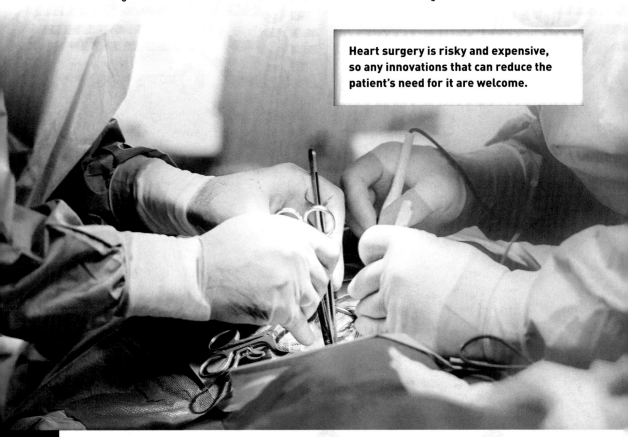

Heart surgery is risky and expensive, so any innovations that can reduce the patient's need for it are welcome.

Faulty Valves

The heart works like a pump. It is made of a group of muscles and blood vessels that pump blood to and from the lungs and all around the body. To control the flow of the blood, the heart contains some valves. These are flaps that open to let the blood through, then close again to keep it from flowing back the wrong way. Sometimes, these valves stop working properly. They can be either repaired or replaced, but both procedures require major surgery. The patient has a large cut made down their chest so the surgeon can reach their heart. Innovative surgeons, however, have now devised a way to replace one of the heart's valves in a much less invasive way. They can reach and replace the valve in one of the major blood vessels, called the aorta, through an opening that is 2 inches (5 cm) long instead of about 10 inches (25 cm). Patients recover much more quickly from this operation, and are soon back on their feet.

INGENIOUS INNOVATIONS

Heart disease in low-income countries is increasing as people are living longer. Yet there are few trained heart specialists to look after them. One innovator from Cameroon, Arthur Zang, came up with a device to help address this problem. This is CardioPad, a medical tablet that allows health care workers in remote areas to send the results of tests to heart specialists via a cell phone connection. CardioPad has wires and sensors that attach to the patient and collect data on their heartbeat. The experts then reply with treatment advice.

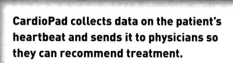

CardioPad collects data on the patient's heartbeat and sends it to physicians so they can recommend treatment.

27

ReDS

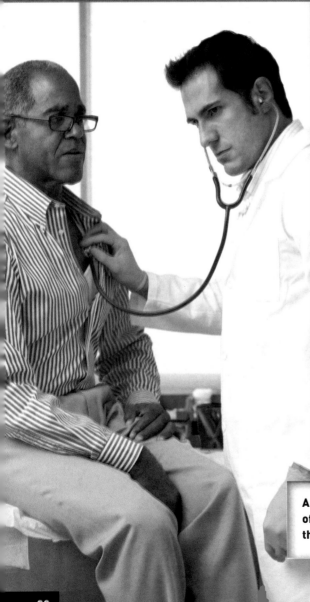

One of the symptoms that people with heart disease experience is difficulty breathing. This can make everyday life difficult, by reducing their ability to move around comfortably. One recent innovation, called the ReDS, is designed to address this problem, by taking a closer look at what is going on.

Patients with heart disease experience difficulty breathing because there is fluid building up in their lungs. This happens because their heart is not pumping strongly enough to keep up with the body's needs and to shift any fluid that collects there. Until now, cardiologists have not been able to see how much fluid was in the lungs, and whether that amount was increasing, without an invasive procedure.

A doctor listening to the breathing of a patient with heart disease can hear the fluid that has built up in their lungs.

Wear It

Amir Ronen trained as an electrical engineer in Israel. His research in medical technology led him to set up a company called Sensible Medical, which aims to bring top-level technology innovations to the area of heart-failure care. At Sensible Medical, they developed the ReDS. Patients wear this high-tech vest and it measures the amount of fluid in their lungs, from outside their clothing. It does this using a technology called radar, which was first used by the military, and by rescue teams to see through walls and rubble in collapsed buildings. Radar uses radio waves to see through the chest wall and build up a picture of what is inside the lungs. Sensible Medical has miniaturized that technology, and built it into the ReDS, to get an accurate measurement of fluid in the lungs.

Early Warning

There are many advantages to the ReDS. It can be used in hospitals to give doctors accurate information, so they can decide on the best treatment to reduce the amount of fluid. Patients can also use it at home. They may experience rapid changes in the amount of fluid they carry in their lungs and even small increases can make them feel much worse. Being able to check their lungs every day gives them peace of mind when all is well, and the evidence to take action if it is not.

The simple test takes just 90 seconds, and the results go automatically to their physician at the hospital, who monitors them for any worrying changes. So far, research suggests that patients using the ReDS are less likely to need to return to the hospital. Their treatment can be adapted before they become very sick. This early-warning system is working very well, and it is becoming a valuable tool in the treatment of heart disease around the world.

Amir Ronen's ReDS device gives patients the freedom to monitor their condition at home, and get expert advice when they need it.

CHAPTER 5

ANTIBIOTIC RESISTANCE

Antibiotics are drugs that treat infections. These can be anything from an ear or throat infection to a serious disease. The problem we face is that we have become so good at using antibiotics to fight diseases that the diseases are fighting back. The bacteria that cause the diseases are adapting and finding ways to survive the antibiotics—or becoming resistant to them. Our drugs are becoming less effective. Scientists are working to find solutions to this problem, which is one of the biggest facing medicine today.

Some bacteria, like these, have become resistant to the antibiotics we have been using for decades.

Superbugs

The experts fear that if we cannot find ways to fight antibiotic resistance, we can expect up to 10 million more people to die each year by 2050. Fortunately, individuals, researchers, institutions, and governments around the world are working together on innovations to combat the threat from these resistant "superbugs."

In the United States, the CDC is responding to the problem with a network called the Antibiotic Resistance Lab Network (AR Lab Network). It has labs around the country, tracking resistance and sharing data with the hospitals, doctors, and scientific institutions that are developing tests

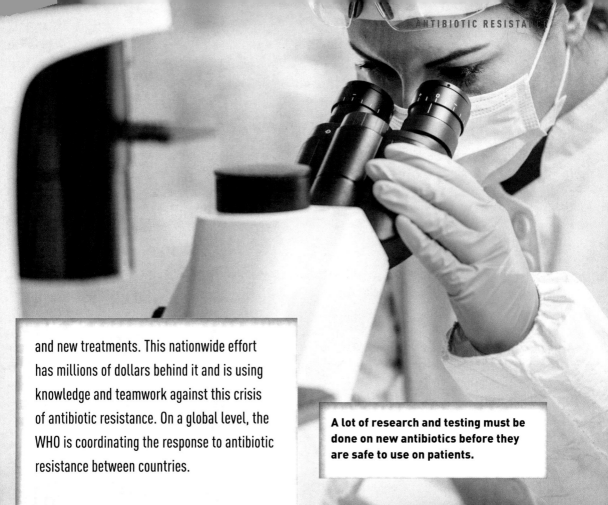

and new treatments. This nationwide effort has millions of dollars behind it and is using knowledge and teamwork against this crisis of antibiotic resistance. On a global level, the WHO is coordinating the response to antibiotic resistance between countries.

A lot of research and testing must be done on new antibiotics before they are safe to use on patients.

Good Versus Bad

We have billions of bacteria inside us all the time, many of them in our gut. Most of these are good for us and help keep our immune systems healthy. Some scientists think that we could use these good bacteria to help us fight the bad ones that cause disease, without the need for antibiotic drugs. One company in the United States, Vedanta Biosciences, which is based in Massachusetts, is developing drugs based on this idea. Two of its drugs that use good bacteria are ready for trialing, and if they work, it could be a breakthrough.

Sharing Knowledge

Sometimes in medicine, doctors and research scientists do not work together enough to solve problems. Some information can be gained only from working with patients as a doctor. At the Antibiotic Resistance Center at Emory University in Georgia, doctors and research scientists are working together to better understand how to diagnose and treat antibiotic resistance. As a result, they have designed a new test to discover exactly which bacteria are resisting the drugs in real patients.

New Antibiotics

If the antibiotics we currently take are not working, surely we should be developing new ones? Unfortunately, however, hardly any new antibiotics have been created for about the past 30 years. This is because it has not made good business sense for the pharmaceutical companies that make them. Developing a new drug costs millions of dollars, but antibiotics have to be sold at too low a price to earn back those costs. A new solution is needed.

One organization in Philadelphia, Pennsylvania, is working on it. Pew Charitable Trusts has developed the Shared Platform for Antibiotic Research and Knowledge (SPARK). This is an online library of data and research that is freely available to scientists around the world to use, so they can work together on building new discoveries.

Making New Weapons

In recent years, research into new antibiotics has increased because the drug companies have been supported by money from governments and other sources. In summer 2018, a new antibiotic was approved in the United States that can treat a superbug

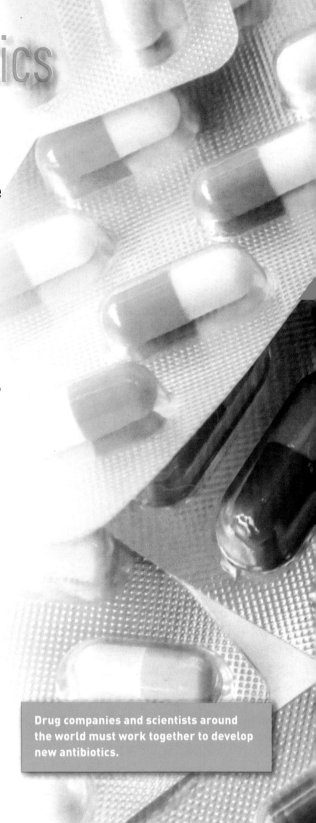

Drug companies and scientists around the world must work together to develop new antibiotics.

that has been resisting other antibiotics. It took more than a decade to get this medicine from promising laboratory research to a safe, approved medicine that patients can use.

There is one powerful antibiotic that doctors use only when all else has failed. This is called vancomycin. Although it has avoided resistance until now, recently bacteria have been found that are resistant to it. Dale Bolger and his team at the Scripps Research Institute in La Jolla, California, are working to change the structure of vancomycin, to make it more effective. The signs are promising so far, and he hopes new versions of the drug can be manufactured before too long.

Teixobactin is a new antibiotic that scientists hope will soon be available for treating infections that can resist other antibiotics.

INGENIOUS INNOVATIONS

In 2015, scientists in the United States discovered a natural antibiotic called teixobactin in soil samples. At the University of Lincoln in the U.K., scientists decided to try to create a simpler, man-made version of teixobactin, which could be used as a treatment. They did this successfully and used it to treat a bacterial infection in mice. They were delighted at the positive results. The infection had resisted the regular antibiotics used to clear it, but teixobactin worked. Now they are working to create a version of teixobactin that can safely be used for people. This could take several years, but it could lead to the first new class of antibiotic drug in 30 years.

Alternatives to Antibiotics

In the fight against the toughest bacteria, one major part of the battle plan is to look for alternatives to antibiotics. Scientists are researching several different areas of biology, and their innovative work is looking promising.

Antibodies

Antibodies are special cells in the immune system that can recognize the harmful bacteria that invade the body and cause disease. They start off the process of destroying them. Researchers at the National Institute of Allergy and Infectious Diseases (NIAID) and the New Jersey Medical School-Rutgers University recently used antibodies, rather than antibiotics, to treat a bacteria called *Klebsiella*. *Klebsiella* causes about 10 percent of all infections caught in hospitals in the United States, and one type of it is resistant to most antibiotics, so it is a big threat. So far this work has been done only in lab test tubes. It will take a long time to develop this line of research, but it looks exciting.

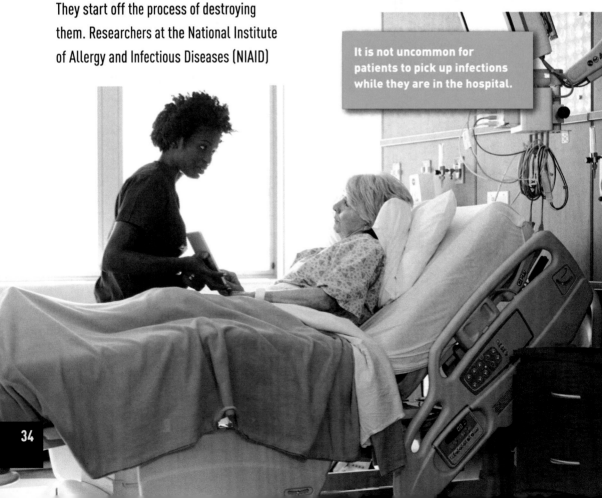

It is not uncommon for patients to pick up infections while they are in the hospital.

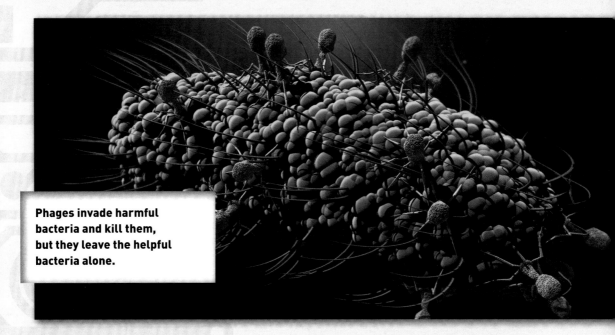

Phages invade harmful bacteria and kill them, but they leave the helpful bacteria alone.

Phages

Another alternative to antibiotics is attracting a lot of attention. This makes use of the most common organisms on our planet, which have been around for millions of years and are part of our everyday life without us knowing it. These are called phages. Phages are viruses that are present in soil, seawater, and inside us. In fact, we have about 1 million billion of them in our gut. In order to reproduce, phages must invade the cells of bacteria and kill them. They break down the walls of the bacteria using substances called endolysins.

Scientists are excited at the idea of using phages and their endolysins to kill harmful bacteria in patients with disease. Phages have several advantages. Each phage kills one type of bacteria, so they can be used specifically for one disease. If the bacteria evolve to resist a particular phage, scientists can find another that attacks it in a different way. This makes it much more difficult for the bacteria to develop resistance. Also, unlike antibiotics, which kill the good and bad bacteria in our bodies, phages do not kill the good bacteria that are beneficial to our health.

The science of using phages was first discovered 100 years ago, but when antibiotics were developed and became widely used from the 1940s, the use of phages almost died out. However, using phages to fight disease is making a comeback and the first large-scale trials have begun. Hopefully, this 100-year-old therapy will help us beat the superbugs.

35

Malacidins

The ground beneath our feet may be dirt, but it could also hold the key to the new antibiotics we so desperately need. One pioneering researcher in the United States has made an important breakthrough by getting his hands dirty.

Citizen Science

Sean Brady is a scientist working in the laboratory at The Rockefeller University, New York. He understood that soil is teeming with microbes such as bacteria, and that some of those bacteria produce substances that can kill the harmful bacteria that cause diseases. In fact, substances derived from those bacteria have been the major source for the antibiotics we use today. But scientists had all but given up on discovering any new antibiotic substances this way. They thought they had found all there was to be found. Brady thought this might not be true, and he and his team thought up a new approach to investigate.

Brady has people power on his side. He asked citizens from across the United States to mail him samples of their local soil. He then found the many, many bacteria in these

Sean Brady's work has led to the discovery of new antibiotics called malacidins.

Different kinds of soil samples were collected and analyzed from around the United States.

samples, and started to analyze their genes. He was looking for a particular mix of genes that he knew were present in some existing antibiotics. What he found was astonishing—about 75 percent of the soil samples contained bacteria that had this mix of genes. This suggested there were many more new antibiotics to be found from among them.

Powerful Drugs

After more work, Brady and his team were able to identify and develop a whole new class of antibiotics from these bacteria. They decided to call them malacidins, which is Latin for "killing the bad." They tested them on infections caused by antibiotic-resistant bacteria—and they worked! This looked like an important new weapon in this dangerous fight.

Was it possible, however, that the bacteria that cause infections would develop resistance to these new antibiotics, the malacidins, as they have to others? Brady and his team put this to the test, but none of the bacteria showed any signs of developing resistance. The malacidins continued to kill them.

Having an effective new antibiotic is great news. Malacidins have not yet been developed for use with patients, but Brady and his team are working toward that goal. He is also sure that the dirt beneath our feet contains many more bacteria that can help us solve this urgent problem.

CHAPTER 6

RECOVERY AND REHABILITATION

One of the most important areas of health care is getting people back on their feet after an illness. They may have had surgery, an accident, or an illness that has kept them in bed for a long period. This work is known as rehabilitation, or rehab for short. It can be slow work and it takes expert care. Innovations are delivering great advances in this important work.

Physical Therapy

People who have had a stroke often lose the ability to use parts of their body fully. Some of this movement can be restored by doing a program of controlled exercises. This is known as physical therapy. Physical therapy is very labor intensive. One, or often two, therapists

INGENIOUS INNOVATIONS

Forms of wearable technology are being developed for rehab. One U.S. company, Seismic, has recently developed a wearable suit that boosts the wearer's muscle power, helping them move and walk. There are tiny motors embedded in the suit at the joints of the body. These "contract" in a way similar to our muscles, providing extra power to the wearer. Sensors in the suit track their movement, telling the artificial muscles when to activate.

The Seismic "supersuit" is lightweight and comfortable. It works with the wearer's muscles to boost their power.

work with the patient for up to an hour at a time, usually several times a day. One way to give patients more therapy is by using robotic aids. Several innovators around the world are working on robotic gloves, for example. These help the wearer move their fingers and hands in a series of exercises. After repeated use, the person relearns how to use their hand and finger muscles, so they can perform everyday tasks.

Virtual Reality

Other innovators are using a technology that most of us think of as a game. This is virtual reality (VR). It can be a powerful tool in rehabilitation because it provides an environment for the patient to practice their exercises and a series of everyday tasks. It gives the patient a training schedule to follow and monitors how they perform. It then uses the data from their performance to design changes to their schedule. Neuro Rehab VR is a young company in Texas that is pioneering training exercises that are finely tailored to meet the abilities and goals of each different user.

Physical therapy delivered to the patient by VR is showing promising signs of success.

Back on Your Feet

Millions of people around the world lose limbs as a result of accidents or disease. The problem is especially severe in poorer countries. There are many more road accidents in these places than in wealthier countries, often causing limb loss. People also lose limbs through disease because medical care may be ineffective. Replacement limbs are called prosthetics. The WHO estimates there are about 30 million people needing prosthetic limbs or other mobility devices, but they have traditionally been expensive and complex to make.

3-D printed hands like this one are transforming the lives of thousands of people who have lost a hand.

Give Me a Hand

One new technology that is transforming all this is three-dimensional (3-D) printing. Ivan Owen is a U.S. artist who used to make puppets until, one day, he started using 3-D printing to make a small hand for a boy he heard of who had no fingers on his right hand. He designed the hand, and then he put the templates, or designs, online for anyone to use. This grew into Enabling the Future, a network with 7,000 members across the world who now make arms and hands for people who have lost these limbs.

Jorge Zuniga is a research scientist at the University of Nebraska Omaha. He heard about this and started designing hands for children, too. His project, Cyborg Beast, designs 3-D printed hands that look like robot parts, as this is what the children like best. His design is freely available online and has been downloaded more than 48,000 times. Anyone with access to a 3-D printer can now have a cheap and life-changing hand in minutes.

Nursebots

When patients return home from the hospital, they usually need extra help with getting back into their everyday routine safely. It is often not practical or affordable for them to have a nurse live with them, but innovators have developed the next best thing, nursebot. This robot is a personal assistant that helps with daily tasks and provides a little companionship. Nursebot can recognize the speech of its owner, and can follow them around. A touchscreen on the robot's front can give instructions. For example, nursebot can remind her owner to take their medication, to attend an appointment, or to do rehabilitation exercises.

Pearl is a nursebot. She can remind people to attend appointments or take medication, and record their movements.

Robotic Rehab Suit

Conor Walsh is a professor of engineering at Harvard University. He is the founder and leader of the Harvard Biodesign Lab, where he and his team have worked on some remarkable innovations. These innovations have won him more than 30 professional and public awards and prizes. One of his most amazing innovations is his robotic rehab suit.

Conor Walsh tested and adapted his comfortable robotic suit many times until it worked perfectly.

Walsh was born and educated in Ireland, but when he developed a passion for robotics he knew he would have to move to the United States, where much groundbreaking robotics work was being done. The first projects he saw for robotic suits were quite promising, but the suits were stiff, heavy, and uncomfortable. He knew that he wanted to design one that was easier to wear because, if it were comfortable, it would be much more likely to be used by the patient, and therefore be successful. Walsh teamed up with some experts in clothing design to make a different kind of suit. Now millions of people who have suffered a stroke or have other mobility problems may one day walk confidently again thanks to his soft robotic rehab suit.

Soft and Comfortable

The suit, worn under normal clothes, is equipped with tiny yet powerful motors, pulleys, cables, movement sensors, and intelligent software. It can immediately read what the wearer is trying to do, and assist them to walk better by making gentle corrections and encouraging natural physical actions. It gives patients more stability and more confidence as they move. Walsh says his patients love it: "They say it takes the process of walking out of your head. You just get on and do it."

The suit can be worn in the patient's own home, so they can carry on exercising even beyond the clinic. It can still be monitored by the therapists remotely, so it can be adjusted to suit the patient's changing needs.

Spreading the Word

Conor Walsh is passionate about educating future innovators. He has established the Harvard Medical Device Innovation Initiative. This provides students with the opportunity to collaborate with physicians in Boston and in low-income countries, such as India. In addition, his research group has launched the Soft Robotics Toolkit. This is an online resource, freely open to all, to share materials for soft robotics.

> The suit works with the wearer, so that their assisted movement ends up feeling natural.

INNOVATORS OF THE FUTURE

The world of cutting-edge medicine sometimes seems rather like science fiction. In surgery, for example, robotic devices are helping surgeons perform ever-more delicate procedures on the body. Organ transplants have become routine, but in 2018, French surgeons performed the first ever double face transplant, after a patient's body rejected the transplant he had received 10 years earlier.

Precious Eyes

Our eyesight is precious, and scientists know it. In the U.K., Oxford University researchers have found a way to restore the sight of some people who inherited a serious eye disease, with a therapy that alters their genes. The genes they are missing are injected into the back of their eyes. At Harvard, they have invented a new kind of contact lens that slowly releases medication into the eye as it is worn. This is an all-new way to treat some eye diseases.

Advances in understanding how our genes work are leading to some of the most exciting medical innovations.

Drug Delivery

Delivering drugs to the body is an important area of innovation in other ways, too. Robotics and medicine are coming together to devise tiny robots, called nanobots. These are small enough to be injected into a patient's blood and can travel around the body. They can be used to deliver medications to exactly where they are needed, reducing the amount of damage to surrounding areas. This is particularly useful in treating cancerous tumors, because the medications are powerful and can harm surrounding healthy areas.

Cancer

In the fight against cancer, scientists are pioneering the use of artificial intelligence (AI). This uses machines to collect data from patients' tumors, detect patterns in that data, and "learn" what might happen next.

New techniques can pick out patterns in how different kinds of tumors change as they grow bigger. With that knowledge, they can predict how a tumor may develop, and so give physicians more time to find the best treatment for it. This is treatment personalized for each individual patient, and it is an important trend in medical innovation.

Finding a Way

There is almost no limit to the exciting advances being made in the field of medicine today. Around the world, scientists, companies, and governments are working hard to deliver better health care to more people. The resources we have are being put to better use, and innovative ways are being found to deliver more care for lower costs.

Nanobots are being developed to deliver drugs and carry out procedures in areas of the body that we could not otherwise reach.

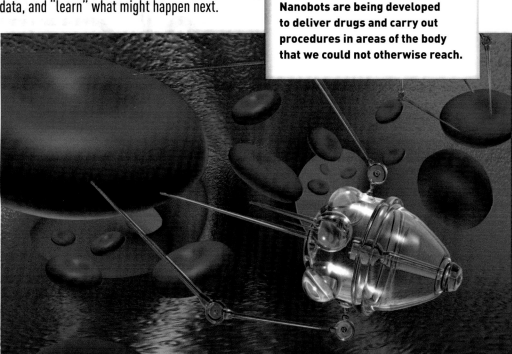

Glossary

antibiotics drugs that treat infections

antibodies body cells that can fight bacteria

artificial intelligence (AI) programs that allow computers to learn and make decisions

bacteria tiny living things that can cause disease

biomedical relating to the body and to medicine

blood vessel a tube that carries blood through the body

cancer a disease that causes harmful growths called tumors in the body

data information

developed world wealthy countries where most people have good living conditions

developing countries poorer countries that are trying to improve people's living conditions

diabetes a disease that causes too much sugar in the blood

diagnosing identifying the nature of an illness

eco-friendly not harmful to the environment

genes instructions in the cells of living things that control their characteristics

immune system the system in the body that fights infection

impaired damaged

inaccessible difficult to reach

infectious easily passed on to other people

invasive entering or cutting into the body

low-income earning little money

microbes tiny organisms such as bacteria

organ a body part that carries out a particular function, such as the heart or brain

organisms living things

pacemaker a device to regulate the heartbeat

phage a tiny living thing that invades the cells of bacteria in order to reproduce

pharmaceutical to do with making drugs

pneumonia a serious disease of the lungs

portable easy to carry

prosthetic a man-made body part

radar a system that sends out radio waves, which bounce off objects and return, building a picture of the surroundings

rehabilitation the process of restoring someone to a normal life after they have been unwell

remote far away or difficult to reach

resistance fighting against attack

sensors devices that measure heat, sound, light, movement, or other physical properties

software a program that gives a computer a set of instructions to perform particular tasks

superbugs bacteria that are not killed by medications normally used against them

transplants when organs or other body parts from one body are put into another

trialed carefully tested

tumors abnormal lumps of cells in the body

vaccines substances that give protection against a disease

virtual reality (VR) an environment produced by a computer that is so realistic it seems to be part of the real world

X-rays photographs of the inside of the body

For More Information

Books

Biskup, Agnieszka. *Medical Marvels: The Next 100 Years of Medicine.* North Mankato, MN: Capstone Press, 2017.

Eboch, M.M. *The 12 Biggest Breakthroughs in Medicine.* North Mankato, MN: 12-Story Library, 2015.

Kovacs, Vic. *Antibiotics.* New York, NY: Gareth Stevens Publishing, 2017.

Latta, Susan M. *Bold Women of Medicine: 21 Stories of Astounding Discoveries, Daring Surgeries, and Healing Breakthroughs.* Chicago, IL: Chicago Review Press, 2017.

Websites

Discover more groundbreaking medical innovations at:
kidsahead.com/subjects/17-medical-innovations

Find out more about how technology is improving health care at:
www.factmonster.com/dk/encyclopedia/science/medical-technology

Learn about future technologies in the field of medicine at:
www.futureforall.org/futureofmedicine/medical_technology.htm

Publisher's note to educators and parents:
Our editors have carefully reviewed these websites to ensure that they are suitable for students. Many websites change frequently, however, and we cannot guarantee that a site's future contents will continue to meet our high standards of quality and educational value. Be advised that students should be closely supervised whenever they access the Internet.

Index